D0948124

REMIND ME THAT I'M WILD

Written by: Tera Freese
Illustrated by: Lindy Kehoe

THE MASTERKEY PRESS ASHEVILLE NORTH CAROLINA

2014

Remind Me That I'm Wild

Copyright January 2014 by Tera Freese

CREDITS

Artwork by: Lindy Kehoe
Edited by: Barton Sutter
Typesetting/design/layout by: Tera Freese & Melissa Warp

E-mail: tera.freese@yahoo.com
ISBN: 978-0-9915068-8-0   Print
Website: www.remindmethatiamwild.com
Published by: The Master Key Press: www.masterkeypress.com

COPYRIGHT:

Contact the above address to order, or call/fax/e-mail for more information about this book.

To the Wild beauty in each one of us!

&

To Maria and Scarlet, of course.

Remind Me That I'm Wild

Down at the bottom of this dark well
an icy raven sits
and next to him another and another,
there are six–

With chants and charms and feathers
and beaks much sharper than most,
their circle holds through frigid weather
and I do not mean to boast–

But they know my name and knew my
others
before I was this child–
yes they keep my secrets and give me power
and remind me that I'm wild–

Down at the bottom of this dark well,
the shining eyes of my kin–
One wears my new red glasses
(they fell when I peered in.)

The Magic That Wakes You

The magic that wakes you at 3 AM
The magic that tells you to pull out your pen,
Your pencils, your sketchbook, your tubes of paint
To capture the dreamland from which you came–

Tell about the pink door you could walk through
Draw the turquoise hills above which you flew
The tangerine breeze, the purple deep
Yes, it's true that you do need your sleep

There's school in the morning, piano and chores
Don't toss in your bed feeling so torn –
For the cat with the gold eyes has something to say
She visited you — and this is the way

All poems, all songs, stories, paintings are born –
It's the magic that wakes you at 3 in the morn.

Theater in the Woods

We've made a theater in the woods
and though it isn't Broadway–
There's a blooming willow curtain
and we sure do hope you'll stay

on our genuine stone seats
or a tree stump if you'd rather–
We've spruced and softened them
with all the green moss we could gather–

We've quite an orchestra–
two ukuleles and a fiddle
and Dad gave us three feed pallets
for stages right, left and middle–

The sun will do our lighting
the chickadees, our sound
two well- groomed squirrels are ushers
and our actors are just bound

to hold your attention, steal your heart,
tell a swell, swooning tale–
Shall we send you off four tickets
right now – in the mail?

The show will start at 3:43
the last Friday of September
We've costumes to sew from spider's silk
 a zillion lines to remember–

Just take the skinny trail
to the thousand year old pine–
Oh, we do think you will find
our show to be divine.

Flying Instructions

Stand on one foot
Raise your right knee
Focus on your third eye
If you had one, I mean-

Spiral your spine
And you'll soon be levitatin'
Orbit your hips
You're liftin' and elevatin'

Propel and spin your arms
Like a helicopter flying
Believe – believe – believe –
Or what's the use in trying?

Unicycle

A unicycle on a dirt road
is a silly thing indeed –
Before I can touch the peddles,
my mouth is full of weeds!

And when after hours of trying
I finally make one circle round –
A rock quickly trips
and lands me on the ground.

I've a scrape on my chin, a bloody knee
and dust in my underwear
and don't forget my favorite jeans
have eighty three new tears!

Yes there's ruts and stones and potholes
I'm covered with mud, I'm frazzled, I'm mad!
I'd throw it in the ditch, I would
and I'm tellin' you I'd be glad–
But the person who gave me this unicycle
Is my very own DAD!

Don't Go

You might be tempted -same as me-
to take the other route
Away from the lines of buses and cars,
the rumbling engines, the horns that shout-

The one that climbs through thin white birches,
the one that winds and winks at the moon
I'm telling you – don't go-
Not yet – it's too soon.

For the fairies will enchant you–
write their names in silver ink
all over your arms, your feet, your face
and you won't be able to think

Of anything but getting back
to their echoing canyon, their moss stitched room-
Take it from me and don't go
Not yet - it's too soon.

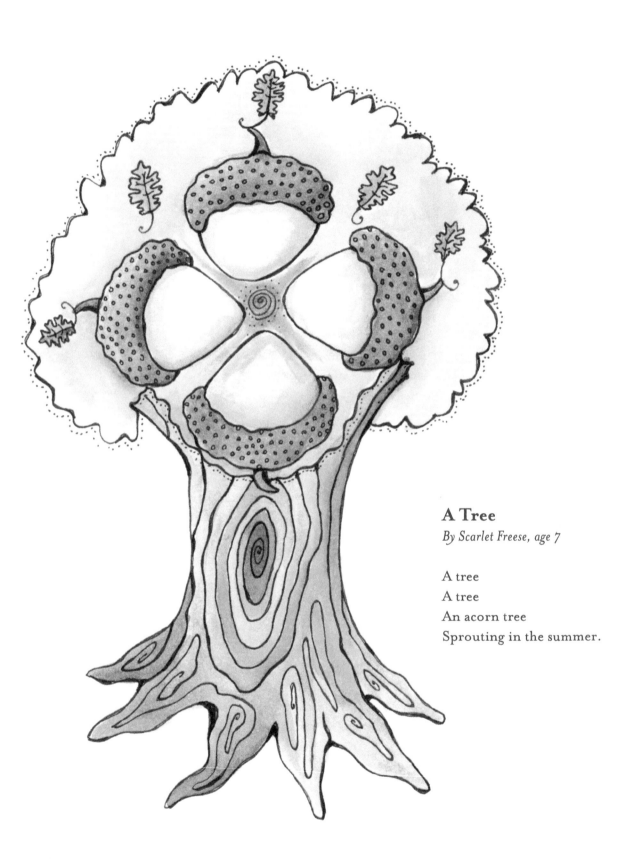

A Tree
By Scarlet Freese, age 7

A tree
A tree
An acorn tree
Sprouting in the summer.

Green Couch

Springy as moss
A fairy trampoline!

A pile of pillows
Jumpy feet
Higher than you've ever seen!

We've got wings
So the only thing missing
Is the sky and stream!

Brave Crossing

I can only wonder how she'll cross
that stretch of bog between the wood
where the grasses grow in wiley tufts
like hair rising from a cone shaped hood

One stumble and she's sure to wake the slimy somethings sleeping
In the slippery stink below where my little sister is now leaping

From patch to patch she hops
Like a pen following a dot to dot
I should ring the bells, clash the cymbals, cry out
BEWARE THE SNARLED TOOTH CROC!

but I just sit and watch – speechless really–
from the safety of this rock.

Way Back Where the Cedars Grow

I'm telling you I can make it
If my legs are strong and steady
If I've half a gallon of water and
My mind is clear and ready

I only need a change of clothes,
Some cashews and some sweets,
A detailed map, a good night sleep,
A lightweight tent and a few more treats

And don't forget a head lamp
A small goat to show the way,
A deck of cards, a bag of gummies
Some underwear and half a day!

I've heard the trail is all uphill
That the wind never ceases to blow
(and it's true this will be my twenty-ninth attempt to go-)
But I can make it — I can make it-
Way back where the cedars grow.

Agate Hunt

A pebbled beach
bright morning land
I search
for twinkling eyes in sand

An icy lake
lyric of the loon
A silver stone
dropped from the moon!

The Forest Has Lessons 'A Plenty

Go ahead and memorize
math facts, verbs, treaties, wars–
Navigate the land of screens
that this new world adores–

But please also study the river's forgotten lore.

The wild ferns, the rapids
The stones all slippery under your shoe–
The gnarled and twisted cedar root,
The moss and red clay, too–

Yes the forest has lessons 'a plenty for you.

Go ahead and google this
Twitter, text and zoom–
Exercise your thumbs, but also
Gaze up at the moon–

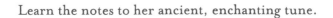

Learn the notes to her ancient, enchanting tune.

Set up a lab by the creek side
Test the water, watch a trout–
This is what science and nature
Are really all about–

And the water is a teacher that I'm sure you'll never doubt.

Of course, school is important,
I did not mean to say otherwise–
But so is the starlit journey
The trails, the hills that you climb–

Enter the forest and you'll see what I mean with your very own eyes.

Stuck In My Head

I've a song stuck in my head
For the last eleven days
It's bare feet on crunchy leaves
A tambourine wave
Down come the pine needles
Shake   Shake   Shake
And at night its melody
Is keeping me awake-

The words are kinda muffled
A foggy spring beach
When the clouds sink low to say hello
When the lake rises to greet
When you can't see the house from the road
Or your head from your feet
This song rolls like mist through my skull
Week after week after week-

Its been running like a river
Quick silver fish, water snake–
Splashing in swimming holes
Canoeing rapids, hook and bait–
I should be working on my speech
My projects sure to be late–
But sun bathin' on lily pads
Seems my musical fate
This songs been in my head ten years
And – to think – I'm only eight.

A Bit of Magic

The trees are brown
And so's the ground
The ice too thin for skating

You watch the skys
Cold steely eye
For flurries and flakes you're waiting

With head bent low
In your red wool coat
With hands tucked deep inside

Shuffling slow
Just watching the road
And the rock you kick aside

A glimmer, a wink
A silver streak
Pick it up in your hand

This swirling agate
Is a bit of magic
From November's frozen land.

If You're Invited to the North

If you're invited to the north,
that cold part of the globe
where there's no use in trying to blow
the frozen gunk from your nose
and where the arctic air is sure to freeze your toes-

If you're invited to the north
do pack your skinny skis
for following the frozen creek
that gurgles and groans beneath your feet
and a backpack with hot tea, chocolate and cheese-

Don't be surprised as you climb and get warmer
if a troll grows from a snowy boulder,
if a fairy melts from an icicle or a crow lands on your shoulder
and whispers secrets that you'll recall even when you're older-

If you're invited to the north
where the wind chills turn lips blue
Do pack up your woolies, your long underwear and don't forget your new
parka that keeps you warm to negative 82!
Grab your sled, don't look back, follow the white hills through and through
(By the way, I invite you!)

Kate's Gate to Heaven

Is up a wintry trail
Beyond the midnight sun and the comet's ta

Where the pines are tall and many
Where there's caution signs a plenty

Where the snows are deep
Where the hills are steep

And a skier must be clever–
Where she'd gladly stay forever!

28

Winter Solstice

Plump orange, studded with clove stars
Fur lined hoods, cold night, bright Mars

We tie together red ribbons, mark a circle on the ground
We've woven holly wreaths to wear as crowns

Out of the quiet, one jingling note of song
Ankle bells, wrist bells join along

Stomp a spiral path into the snow
Weave frosty breath into the unknown

Write a promise in the air with mittened hand
Watch candle lights hum over dark land.

Invite the Wind In

Invite the wind in for coffee,
the door blows open anyway-
Invite the wind in for peppermint tea
on this cold and snowy day.

For she's been all around the globe
through tundras and islands of coconut groves-
along mazes of sea ice, over elephant's backs
in high hills above tree line where the people pack
their homes on the back of their favorite pet yak.

Invite the wind in for soup
and she'll soon fill up the room
with bells, with flags, with golden hoops
spinning to a far far faraway tune.

She makes waves on the ocean and pushes the sails
of a thousand, no a million small boats and the tails-
Yes the tails of the kites that she lifts from the ground
as the children hold tight, the string is unwound-
Those colorful kites are some fifty feet long
that's wider than your house and oh are they strong!

But not quite as strong as the lizards that thrive
in the long sandy deserts where the wind likes to fly-
With no buildings to stop her, no mountains, no trees,

she won't stop blowing for nineteen weeks
and at 200 mile per hour break neck speeds-
and the mouths of those lizards are so packed with sand
they look as if they are a part of the land.

So even though your mom says to close
That door through which the frigid air blows-

If I were you I'd invite the wind in-
give her an open armed hug and a grin
For she's been all around the globe
and will tell a good story once she's unfroze.

School Is Closed

School is closed because of icy roads
You think I'm happy, I suppose
But today our class had library
and of my dragon books I've finished three
and on the last one you must know
I've only just four pages to go
and at recess we're digging tunnels
through the mounds and mounds of snow–
School is closed because of icy roads
You think I'm happy I suppose
But I made a new friend with a wonderful smile
and now she can't come after to play awhile!

Letters To Maria
By Maria Freese, age 9

Dear Maria,
I am falling past your shoulder–
Look quickly
and you'll see me
and my patterns,
but soon I will be buried in the snow.

Very Truly Yours,
The Snowflake

Dear Maria,
I wish the moss
growing on me would
grow more quickly
so I could warm up.

Very Truly Yours,
The Curvy Log

Dear Maria,
Good Morning,
I can't talk for long
unless you brush the snow off me
because I'm using all my strength
to hold myself up.

Very Truly Yours,
The Bunchy Flower

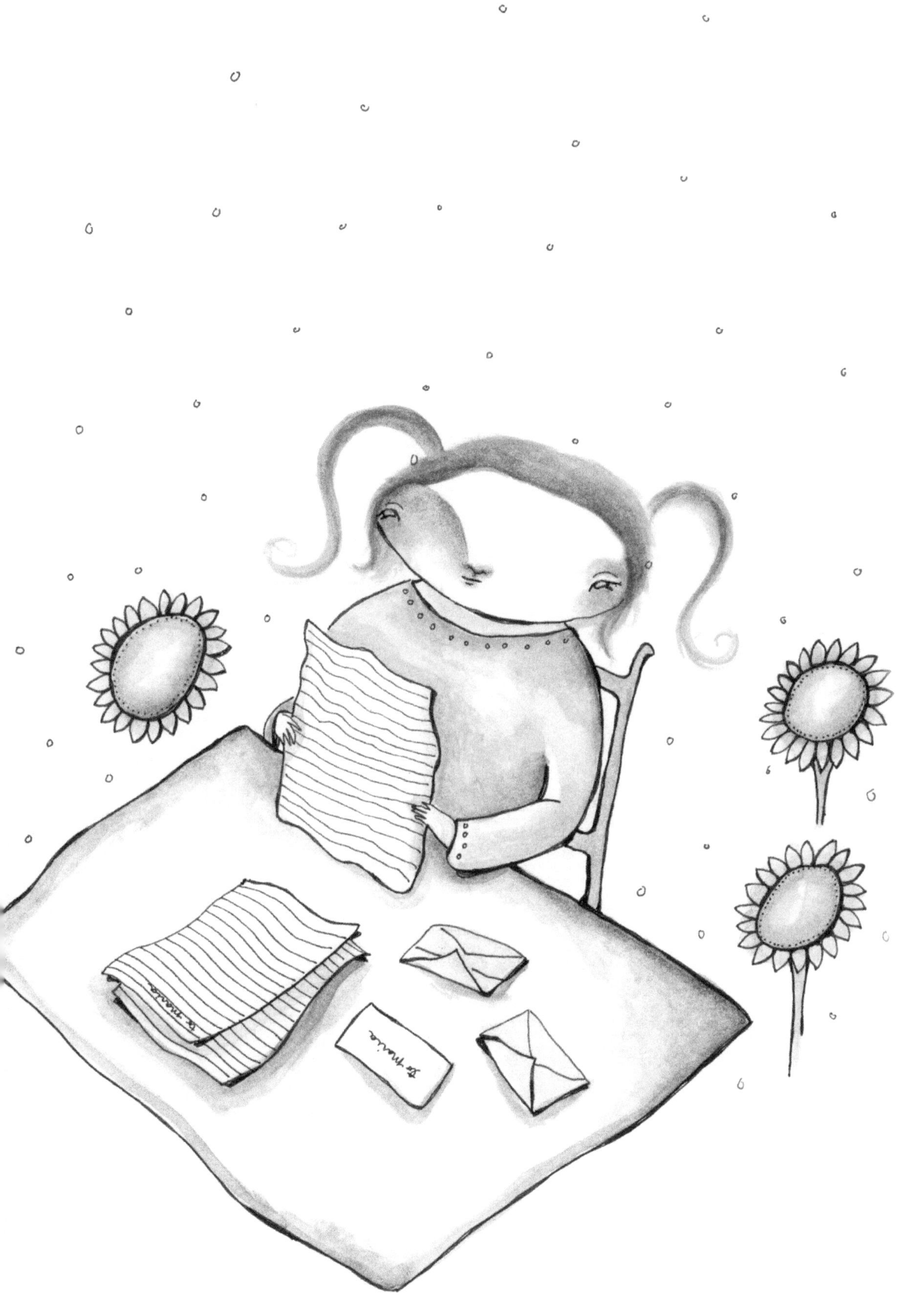

Winter Red

Dogwood spikes like porcupines
Mountain ash berry
A lone cardinal by the feeder
The only red we see

I think that winter is like hide and seek
No flaming maples, no wild rose
On hands and knees we search the wood
A flash of wing, the fire's coals.

Dreaming of June

The creek's thin trail does not now run
Ice not yet freed to water's tune
Oh yellow bangle of the sun–
Come back soon! Come back soon!

The Moon Wins

I stick out my tongue at the moon
because I cannot rest -
She peeks beneath my shade,
wins every staring contest.

For she never blinks, never smiles,
never laughs 'til she almost pees her pants-
She never makes googly eyes,
puffs her cheeks, does a wiggly dance.

She just peers through my window,
through my curtains of lace
And though I try every trick that I know,
She only stares back with her blank white face.

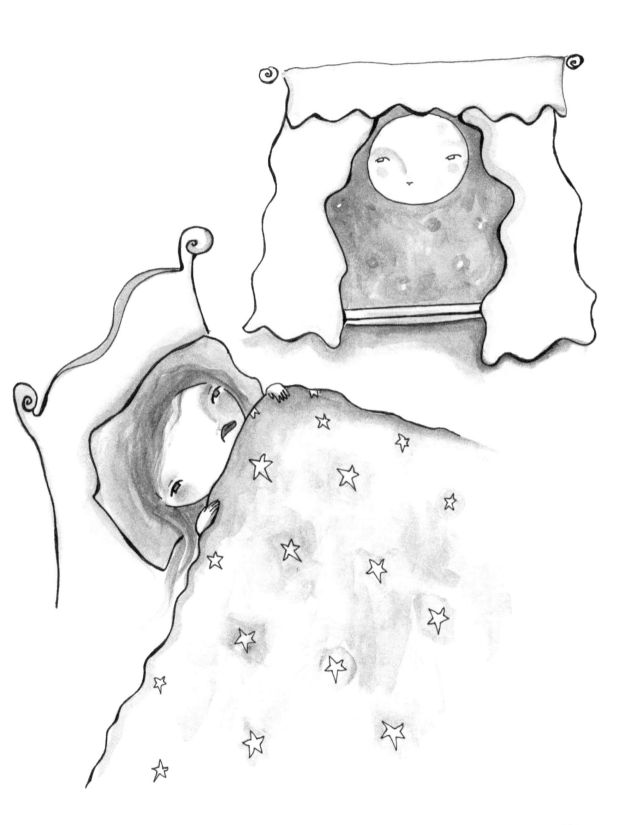

Tulip

I'm only here for a little while
Though I come without fail
I spend quite a bit of time
Underground
Reading nature's braille

Of ice droplets bursting
One by one
Feeling dirt oozing and
Warming from the sun

Wiggling of the earthworms
Helping to make room
For me to climb and burst
Into this scarlet bloom!

March Storm

The morning is all wind
bending cedars
The lake, a grey eye
watching the restless sky.

No one can run as fast as I
A flash of light, cape flies behind–
Water's wild gait pulls boats under,
Rising from my throat, spring thunder!

Northern Spring

We're a cartwheelin' caravan
Somersaulting clowns
Icicles fall from rooftops
Sun is streamin' down–

We've unzipped our jackets
A pile of hats is on the ground
We're celebratin' with some wild
high pitched canine sounds–

This mud is a joy
These puddles are makin' our day
We had a blizzard just last week
and it's the first of May!

Bird Nest

This morning, my mama said
you have a bird nest in your head–
And then I heard a sudden crack
a small beak tap tap tap tap tap
and then the smooth blue feathered back

It seemed that all of nature came so near
as when in a seashell the ocean echoes clear,
the fluttering wing so near my ear.

Then mother saw my funny grin,
checked my web of hair and said–
It looks as if those birds have left their tangled home
flown south or north or east or west–
now run and get a comb!

Helloooooo

I call to the night
To the fox strutting the fields,
to the echoes, the shadows, the loon
Hello to the zillion stars, to the swirling twirling planets,
to the whirling hunks of moon.
Hello to the river that croons.

Helloooooo
I call to the night
To the toads beneath the stairs,
to the hedgehogs and agates and marigolds
and to the snowshoe hares.

Hello to the moss, to the sprouting carrots,
to the caterpillar cozy in her cocoon-
I holler and kick up my heels and shout
this wonderful zany tune-

Helloooooo
I call to the night
So sorry for all of the hullaballoo
But did you...did you know...
IT WILL BE MY BIRTHDAY SOON!

Tree

This is the way I fall
To wet, brown river pieces
To golden raft pieces
To red big as your hand pieces
The winds come and I lose them
all.

This is the way I stand
Brown, bare, silent
Stretching silver maze of silent
Surrounded by forests of white silent
As the snows cover the land

This is the way I bring
Soft pearly stitches of buds
Wet fragrant blousy buds
Prickly sticky mammoth buds
In a great green ring.

This is the way I delight
Web of climbing branches
Heavy with fruit branches
Rope swinging, fort building
branches
In a warm golden light.

You Aren't Who They Say You Are

You aren't who they say you are,
you're ever so much more than that
nose picker, cry baby, poor speller,
child who always talks back–

You're a constellation of stars
with a heart as big as the moon–
You're a warrior, a dreamer, a tree climbing seeker,
an actor, a skater, a player of tunes–

You're as vast and mysterious as the milky way
as fresh and clear as a green spring day–
You're a whistler, a runner and a friend,
a stone throwing swimmer with a message to send–

No you aren't who they speak of behind closed
doors,
not a moping, ungrateful, irresponsible brat–
You and I both know that you're not
now just stop acting like that!

Nature

I'm the wind that breaks the icicles
The witch's frosty breath
The ripples on the face of snow
The bones that tell of death

I'm the heat that warms the soil
The flower bells that ring
The stones that roll, the waves that curl
The green that sings of spring.

I Gave Away

I gave away my tiger's eye,
my shark tooth and my jade–
I gave away my hawk talon,
my mermaid tear, the rings I made–

I gave away my arrow head,
my eagle feather, my slice of sea–
all of them to my best friends–
who needed them more than me.

Tera Freese lives in the woods of northeastern Minnesota with her husband, Paul and two daughters, Maria and Scarlet. She is trying to teach herself and her children to live simply, mindfully and joyfully. There is no place she'd rather be than on a trail where something magical always seems to happen!

Lindy Kehoe is a painter and poet living on the Rogue River in Southern Oregon. Her illustration work with Star Hawk, *The Last Wild Witch* was awarded the Silver Nautilus in 2009. Her work expresses the child-heart in a whimsical and uplifting way. More of her images can be seen at www.lindykehoe.com